T0273414

THIRD MAN BOOKS

OUTSIDE THE JOY

poems

RUTH AWAD

for my mother

THIRD MAN BOOKS

For more information:
Third Man Books, LLC
623 7th Ave S
Nashville, Tennessee 37203

A CIP record is on file with the Library of Congress.

Words and cover design by Ruth Awad
Art direction by Jordan Williams
Design by Amin Qutteineh

ISBN: 979-8-98661-459-5

Contents

All This Wonder

The Whole Red World

Reasons to Live

Because if you can survive
the violet night, you can survive

the next, and the fig tree will ache
with sweetness for you in sunlight that arrives

first at your window, quietly pawing
even when you can't stand it,

and you'll heavy the whining floorboards
of the house you filled with animals

as hurt and lost as you, and the bearded irises will form
fully in their roots, their golden manes

swaying with the want of spring—
live, live, live, live!—

one day you'll put your hands in the earth
and understand an afterlife isn't promised,

but the spray of scorpion grass keeps growing,
and the dogs will sing their whole bodies

in praise of you, and the redbuds will lay
down their pink crowns, and the rivers

will set their stones and ribbons
at your door if only

you'll let the world
soften you with its touching.

In the gloaming, in the roiling night

The hurt returns as it always intended—it is tender
as the inside of my thighs, it is as blue too. O, windless,

        wingless sky, show me your empire of loneliness,
let me spring from the jaws of what tried to kill me.

Let me look at your face and see a heaven worth having, all
                your sorry angels falling off a piano bench, laughing.

Do you burn because you remember darkness? Outside
the joy is clamoring. It is almost like the worst day of your life

           is ordinary for everyone else.

The Aneurysm

The doctor describes arteries as walls walls weaken walls bulge

a house in standing water its light in the window a beacon

you could crash into the heart weakens the heart sings

its little siren song over the cliffs like a house bulging

with water each wave carries more out to sea

the sea bulges with hearts the tide slats in

gulls pick at the heart shrapnel on the beach

the hearts want to know who builds a house on the shore like that

my mother is the house my mother is also the waves

The Heart Is Another Country

Where your name
          is the common tongue
I've gone in search

of your sideways tooth,
          the purple roots of your hair.
Let me barter my life

for yours. No one is listening
          anyway. As a child I thought
I was an animal, and now

I'm sure of it. Pacing like the lion
          in his makeshift habitat.
The spectacle of his suffering!

Let me say the true thing:
          I am afraid each time I see you
may be the last time I see you.

Mother Of

an ascending thoracic
aortic aneurysm, right above
the root. First found seven years
ago. The size of a walnut. She could
not work. We painted her red walls white.
Easier to sell. Put her artwork in storage and moved
her to a farmhouse on a hill. Then the symptoms abated.
The aneurysm dormant as a winter bear. We thought we'd been
spared. In summer it's the size of a ruby plum. The way fruit
can ripen. The doctors speak in a language unlike my
mother. Sharp and sterile. A gloved finger draws
a vertical line down the sternum to explain
an open-chest approach. Her heart,
her heart, the mother of my
whole red world.

My Mother Writes Her Will

When the body is not the person
who made me but a task

on someone's list, I think
there is no wonder left in death

except that a piece of paper will make materially
true what she last wanted on this earth:

for her house to go to my sister
and her paintings to me,

and I have tried to imagine it, the first
in the rest of my days without her,

but when I look up the moon
is as freckled as her skin,

I mistake my own hands
for hers.

The Sarah Poems

We give each other a year to find
reasons to live, but it's not even day
one and I have a handful, more than
enough for the both of us: last night
the train heavy on its tracks yowled
in such a discordant way you would've
laughed your ass off, this marvel of man-
made machinery, its tons of machismo,
honking most undignified. Who will notice
if we're gone? How about this: my money
plant actually withers when my bank
account nears $0. Coincidence? I think
not. What about all the dogs we could
rescue and the ones we can't if we're
not here? Think of the sweet mutts
who took a shovel to the head and still
survived. Who will love them like you
will love them? And you haven't
seen the curiosity of hens, how they
bawk and preen and peck and bully,
the small miracle that is an egg every
morning, still warm. Today the nesting
box latch broke and the hens got loose.
There's nothing like bliss of a silly bird
who thinks she's outfoxed her keeper,
puffed there on the maple stump, grooming
her wings, her triumphant saddles. The birds
escape more than I care to admit,

and one day I'm sure I'll find them gone,
like when Dorothea flew over my head
and out into the street and I ran like
I hadn't since middle school gym class,
my lungs barely burning for the adrenaline,
me yelling after this chicken in front
of God and my neighbors in a city
that hasn't even roused yet, me versus
the hen who can't be reasoned with:
But the stray cats will eat you! The hawks
will too! You're everyone's food! Sarah,
maybe we should be like the hen who
thought I might eat her but was tired
from the chase and scared of what's
next, who chose instead to trust
the arms around her would carry
her back home, who laid her head
on my wrist, whose heartbeat begged
my hand for mercy. Have mercy on me,
I don't want to live in a world without you.

❧

Painful, to love someone more than yourself.
To dread with the deep ink of my blood I'll find you gone.

❦

The year you were born, a robin built her nest on the edge
of the chandelier salvaged from an old church that hung
over our porch on Steuben Street in Wausau, Wisconsin.
It seems important to get the details right. The mother,
like all female robins, built the nest from the inside out,
pressing dead grass and moss and twigs and rootlets
into shape with the wrist of her wing. The care it must
take to construct a home on the fingertip of the world!
I could hardly see it; it was so high. And when the wind
picked up, the chandelier would sway just so. You know
where this is going, don't you? The babies hatched one
by one, their mouths wide with the racket of their hunger.
And the wind like all the birds taking flight. And the mother
returning to her young littering the porch, their eyes shut tight.

❧

The Years of Water & Light

In the rowboat I tied her shoes.

                         And the river cussed and spat.

Our feet swelled and our bellies begged.

                         The end is never how you expect.

This is where I lose her:

                         at the shoreline, in sweet water.

We fed wild dogs overripe apples and herring.

                         My hands shine with hunger.

Her hair hung in willow boughs, mine in wild onion.

                         I reel the small fish of time.

The end never happens and always happens.

                         In winter we suet the trees. The cardinals arrive like snow.

I braid her willow hair. I tie her shoes once more.

                         It is winter again. The birches like crooked combs.

Why are you crying?   *Why are you crying?*

Begin but start with the end:

in spring she is pregnant. In summer she is not.

The baby swims in every room.

See where our steps wet the hallway?

That was when we were swept away.

The Chariot

About eight ounces, the weight
of the human heart,
and for all its galloping
my heart is neither the horse
nor the chariot
pulling me through the dead
Capricorn winter,
all tooth and nail,
past the stripping birches
in the failing light,
past the crying cockerels
and empty-bellied nests,
until it's me and the bleating
wind and the wilting scarlet
runners—in the summer
you'll tell me the aorta
is the size of a garden hose,
your aneurysm the size
of a fig. The future is
a season I can't imagine.

Mother Of

Paintbrushes   face down   in the water cup
and the red tendrils   reaching like the summer
she taught me   to swim at the Y—*ear to the water*
and listen!—   the long vowels of children dimming
to a warble under the surface,   almost holy to be held
that way,   my small body lifted   by the water and
my mother's hands, my mother who pulled me from
nothingness into existence as   simply as a brush
tows red across a   canvas until it's an acre of
bowing poppies, red as my lips drawing another
breath,   red as a choir, I want to fill my pockets
with the color my mother made,   to break the red
mountain and eat its red pulp, to pin its red wings
to my back and walk the red desert of my heart
that learned   from my mother   how to live.

Guilt Me

There somehow exists   a world without you
           full of lesser beasts.

The mourning horses came with their laments
               and bridles, nuzzling the window,

their breath obscuring the pane.   I trailed sunlight through a field
      until the horses were bored. And when

        the dog rose from the ditch,
            mine reared like she'd seen a ghost

and furied off, and I flew unbeautifully
      at the speed of her fear, my boot caught in the stirrup,

her hooves inches from my face.
      What animal clings to another and expects to survive it?

I would die this way: acutely aware of my mistakes. My body dragged
      through dust, half the tattoo on my shoulder scraped away.

The living aren't more important   than
               the dead.

After the fall, the dream horses guilt me. I don't know where to go.

Their manes pulling stars into the bedroom,
             their necks wet with sweat,

we are riding

            for the first   bearable day.

The Cypress

is the tree
of mourning
you can see
it in muslim
cemeteries
even today
it was the first
tree to grow
in paradise
and now
it's the last
tree to grow
over the dead
if you cut
a cypress
back it won't
regenerate
in egypt
its wood
built coffins
its verticality
is not unlike
a soul moving
toward another
existence
cypress gets
its name from
cyparissus

whom apollo loved
and who loved
only his companion
the deer struck
mortally by
his own arrow
and in his anguish
even the gods
took pity
and gave him
boughs and
a branched
crown and
an eternity
to grieve

The Happiest People on Earth

I am supposed to be one of them,   a childless woman,
free as a bacchanalian god and equally drunk on an unparalleled
bliss index.   Bearer of no fruit, lineage   thwarting, last-name
withholding crone, maker of expendable income and disposable men.
Won't I think of the economy? It dreamed only of labor.
But I fill my house with the flea-bitten and discarded,   the animals
wary of any nearing hand. Who will push   the wheel if not the young?
My mother says daughters were the greatest   joy of her life—
don't I want   more happiness   than I can bear? Don't I want
something to succeed me? I have mothered   so much already
I will not leave empty handed, and like a mother, I may not live to see it.

We don't talk about children until we do

I come from two songs:
                    milk of my mother, blood of my father.

If you say my name, I expect you to know where I'm from
and the sea that stormed me,

I expect you to kiss me here, here, and

here's the night America made: *Are you my father,* I said,
                    are you my father? And my blood rang out

like some immodest bell, like some guilty bloom.
I don't know my God so I must not know

my mother—she tells me she was too fucked up to start having kids,

and so I kneel before her,
                    I hold her hands that are my hands.

Half of everything I did was wrong:
see there in the curvature of the earth and my hips

that were made to rift but won't.

A body exists on forgiveness.
                    I forgive my body again and again

until it's unrecognizable:

a stalk of knotweed, a barricade of wild violet.

I name each blade for the children we are told to have,

children to inherit our unlivable world—reap now
                    what we have made.

.

Simple Interstellar Dust

All the Oranges of Tripoli

It is not enough for everything to stem
from Lebanon—no, my father contends,
it was Tripoli where oranges first originated,
and if my sisters and I had any doubt—
just look at this Wikipedia entry for oranges,
my father says, his gap-toothed grin widening
not unlike an orange split open, *just look*—
and like magic (whose origins, I'm told,
are also Lebanese), there for the world
to see: unassailable proof that oranges
come not from South China nor Spain
but Tripoli. And I know oranges
belong to everyone and no one,
and I know my father
is not above editing Wikipedia—
did you know Wikipedia
may well have Lebanese roots?—
and his research may be scientifically
unsound, a story heard from an uncle or cousin,
but this is absolutely true: once
there were vast orange orchards in Tripoli,
and when they were in bloom
the whole city smelled like citrus—
it was like a beautiful woman's perfume,
it was like you could smell sunlight,
and during the war and after
and every time Tripoli burned—
imagine the fruit peeled in your palm,

now imagine that fruit is a city—
It was unlike anything, he says,
I'm telling you, anything.

The one where I beg

I'm watching my country admire its teeth. You said there is no God
and I looked up. The scar on your arm is its own sad music, pink ribbon,
the kind of song that makes us want to fuck strangers. There will be no God
when this is over. What gave me the audacity to touch you? The moon
doesn't care. She shows us our teeth every night. She is so chill about
the way we fuck up her space. Tell God to come get me. From a high
enough vantage point, anything looks like begging. Tell that to the dogs!
How they will howl all night long. They think we must be benevolent
beasts too—all the ways we can hurt each other but don't. I say let's call
this touching a truce. Will we still beg when this is over? When I don't
have any teeth left. When you have the bite marks to prove it.
When we pass this quiet between us, hounds for a world on fire.

Amor Fati

Our gods disappoint us, so we make new ones. Some glower like smoke.
Some wheel in suffering like dying stars. Oh, simple   interstellar dust,

you've made us love the fate that yokes us. To be good when living
makes us mean. Say you know what I mean, northern flicker,

small feather of a smaller planet. God who ate   everything,
did this world feed you? There were enough bodies. There were blades

that passed like a stranger in starlight. In some worlds, you're so close
I could kiss you.
                    In some worlds, we keep meeting.

God of six supposedly impossible things: weep of wolves,
a drought of bullets, the claws of a catalpa, a mother's unworry,

a wilderness of blood,   the dead keeping count.

I, too, am rich in things I never asked for.

Guns Won't Feed You, But Hold Out Your Hands

And forget for a moment
the machine is itself alive

and by design
sated with the alien

softness of organ,
the temporary

framework of bone.
Point its muzzle

only at what you are willing
to destroy—

notice your target
and what is beyond it

and beyond
it—your neighbor,

the dog, a child.
A bullet's path

is characterized by hunger:
how far and how long

and how much?
The truth is the mechanics

don't come naturally.
It should take more

than a finger.

It should
destroy you.

Men Compliment Me

Men compliment me like I'm a distant planet
—only they have the good taste to admire its desolate beauty!

O, to reach into the galaxy like it was filled just for you.
One man tells me I look sad and I think too much so

I think about that too. His good intentions.
My freshly bloodied teeth.

The men who scare me most come not like wolves
but like mice and gnaw at the floor beneath my feet.

I was twelve the first time I was called exotic.
Fourteen, a terrorist.

Fifteen when I starved myself to rib
and yellowed skin. Thin as a tomato slice.

I mean a planet eventually plots its own extinction.
An aging empire flies its flag from the moon.

White men say the world is ending. White men
say the world is ending, and she's asking for it.

Mother Of

God bless the Mitsubishi stuck in snow again on I-65S
that traveled great lengths to bring my mother back
to a state she hates with her whole heart because there's
nothing good about Indiana—her words, not mine, though
if I'm being honest, Indiana is the only place I would not
live again, home of my first kiss with my friend's boyfriend—
let's face it, I was not a good friend and probably not
a good kisser—home of the eggs my first-grade class hatched
and home of the chick I adopted with my father's confused
blessing, the chick who would become a rooster hellbent
on crashing the next-door carwash each night, much to
my distant mother's amusement, to remind the good townspeople
we were, in fact, not like other families, and home to my mother
almost never unless you count the short stays at the Budget Inn
one weekend a month. Oh, my mother, I can almost see her
standing in that long driveway now like she'd been summoned,
like she was too cool for an entire geography, all eyeliner and combat
boots, a babe to end them all, an avenging angel for every lost
girl who grew up in an unglamorous place, and when she packed me
and my sisters up in the car that wanted every day to die, she blazed
out of there on its last breath, her hair streaming out the cracked
window like the flag of a ship warning you to stay away.

Everything Will Hurt for a While

And the lie is that I survived because parts of me didn't.
So take all the sorrow you can carry,
like my mother's cabinets of Slim Fast
and Little Debbies and the weight
we would never lose, how we stood
in front of mirrors and men
hoping one would change our minds
and neither did. Look, here, in her letters
and their cursive of longing: *Baby, survive this.*

Listen, I was only sixteen and drunk
on wine coolers and teenage invincibility,
limp over someone's bathtub, I was lifted
lifted into a bedroom and birdsong
erupted in the delirious morning light.
Her letters sigh, *You've lost too much weight.*
Your dad is starting to worry. Her letters remind
me it could've been worse. When I told her what
happened, she asked, *Are you on birth control?*
None of us got what we deserved.

Shame, Abridged

Walk a circle of salt around the bed. A handful
of feathers. This is how to hide
every moment we lived in the ground.

&

When shame becomes the hand that digs its nails into its fist.
When you move it like a muscle just to feel your skin tighten.
I was thirteen. I stood calf-high in meadow grass. Two high school boys
counting each pixel of flesh as I peeled the fabric from my body.
Become a worse animal. Your quills, their eager hands.

&

Here, my armor: a plate of bone beneath my breasts
and your weight on top of it. Your wife and kids waited
at home, but I could feel them, too. The ceiling fan, turning
and turning over, always above you.

&

Like yarrow at your heel. A thousand leaves.

&

Your chest rising the way a bow draws an arrow.
I want to teach this song
to the children we won't make.

&

A lover said, *You can't make me fall in love with you
and just leave.* It was like in the movies.
Knowing I could have him, even then.
His skin wet in that one-room apartment
with no AC in the dead of summer. I wanted
to feel what I couldn't.

❧

I'm learning what it means to be a woman
and take the world out with one bite.
Out of the garden and into the bog.

❧

I am awake as any animal
under the star-wheeled night.
My skin a red slip
I could slick from my back
if I don't get in my own way.

❧

The faucet beads into the basin.
Be the space between each drip.
In the kitchen, his hand on my thigh.

I don't want to be held that way,
but the body is bones and dirt.
You can bury it anywhere.

Nocturne with Teeth

Black lace is a rhetorical choice;
it could be argued
as an invitation my body gave.
No. Let me start over.
It was theft, pure and simple.
I wear it like a drenched gown
on the bank of a river.
In the growl of night.
Like a wolf tied to her moon.
True as my pink tongue
in my mouth.

Standard Candle

A church rises up around what we don't know.
Imagine living in a town that can't be properly measured—

houses inhale and flicker and skirt. There are only
some stars whose brightness we trust: standard candles,

their brilliance and dimness a compass.
I have a compass to find the Qibla;

I have tried to navigate an impossible God.
Imagine how far light will travel in one year,

like the lover who slept on the far reaches of my bed,
her love a kind of distance. I admit I never knew

sunlight takes eight minutes to arrive on earth.
I admit I felt her warmth long after it was given.

If the sun disappeared right now, we wouldn't know
for eight minutes. If God disappeared right now,

we wouldn't know. Astronauts in orbit are told to find
the Qibla according to their capability. Imagine the stars

turning off their lights particle by particle.
The earth too far to reason with.

What will hold you when you are finally
ready to live uncarefully?

The Jinn Who Loved Me

My shadow came to me on horseback, gold

and hair like smoke. I am your jinn,

you are my sha'ir. So we were bound

together. When heaven split apart, we were red

like dregs of oil, we blinked like cattle

shoved into the daylight,

the knife swift and yet to come.

Origin

Three daughters is called a conspiracy,
our father says. We strike like jinns. Feed him
undercooked potatoes. Build a temple to hide from him.

Fill our dressers with illicit satin straps and hems
of flesh-baring potential, sun our shoulders
in dresses our mother stitched from bargain-bin fabric.

Remember the white wool cape pieced with real
fox fur? She looked like royalty—a miner's daughter
raised on rabbit meat. We are the daughters

of scrap and smoke, tiny black dresses stinking
with the love of strangers. We are like our mother,
the night sky locked in our arms like a man who will hurt us.

Learning Arabic

Suspended in
the Teleferique
above Harissa,
I see our salt-white
lady reach for Beirut.
Language is both
the cedar shade
and mountain road,
the bay licking the heels
of Jounieh. My auntie
teaches me the Arabic
word for *cat*. My
American tongue
and bare legs
say I'm Lebanese
only in blood.
She wants me
to learn.
If not for cables,
we would drop
to our deaths.
If not for our blood,
we'd be untethered.
What saves us
is the one
small thing:
a cable,
a call to prayer,

a new word
strung like a pearl
in the mouth
of a girl.

My Sister and I Make a Suicide Pact

I hate it here, in Tennessee, in America,
on earth, she texts. LOL
I'm a bad day away
from jumping off a bridge.
I just need to outlive
my dogs, that's all.

Hahaha I'll join you.
OK but for real, don't go
without me. Remember
when we were kids
we agreed to poison?

But that would be a mess
for the family to clean up.
Better a bridge,
though I worry
the fall would give me
time to regret it

or remember something
I forgot to do.
Or that there's a next world
worse than this.
Or I would somehow
survive and you would not.

I wait for her reply as a police
helicopter circles low
as if to say, *Not even
the sky can save you.*

The Wolf Tells the Magpie

We cry so the pack will come to us.
We tell the version of the story
that lets us live with ourselves.
Time is a direction and there is
only one hour.
I reason with myself because
I'm not unreasonable.
I let the wrong men in.
I send storms to my lover,
small boxes of them.
Come down to me—
I've been crying
as long as I can remember.

The Sleepwalker

Love was a room I kept walking into.

Ink drenched,   star slick,

rusted in a downpour
                of streetlamps,   I hunt my wild God,

        set loose on your winged heels,

howl down   your babel   moon   if it brings one crumb

to my door. I'll wear your scent like an animal
                carries its young, each gentle fang

the last place that
        mourned you.

❧

Come into the light I've made
in short hours before work
where no one can hurt you like
love can hurt you.

❧

My heart goes wherever it pleases.
It followed you to the middle of the road.
It caught a ride out of town because it looked
mischievous and a little dumb. Rolled
the windows down. Sang its sad songs
unabashed, full blast. Crashed into
the guardrail knowing all the words.

◓

After the Argument

We blurred into shapes, our bodies
like a question we kept asking each other.

At the end of our marriage, I held you
like we'd never disappointed each other.

I dreamt of a tunnel dark as a feather.
You saw me circling from an overpass,

a bird that eats only the dead.
I slipped her name into my beak and flew off.

Forgiveness

This is when you
can look away:

the coyotes poured
into the streets

because we left
them water.

You can be convinced
of anything.

Even the wonder.
See the downed wire,

its electric tongue. The thing
that will break you is small.

I open the windows
and my anger

wants attention.
I let it in.

Catalog of the Inalienable

My father said he gave me this country:
        whatever you can mourn,   you can love.

One day I'll step into the light and be devoured.
I will turn it over in my hands,   bewildered.

It will be like that first brisk winter he didn't
        miss wind in olive trees.

I must love my country because I mourn it.
        Agree each hour to   live another one.

It is very American
        to be this sad on a Tuesday.
                        To grow mean

like a boxwood untaming the window.
        I am so greedy now   I want everything.

Marvel the blood.
                      Expect the algae that blooms
an age of ice. Sometimes what you love

will kill you.   It will rough your mouth   like a kiss.

All This Wonder

Mother Of

Forgetting, having done it before, how to coax
from seed the slow-bolting radish winnowing

on my sill, I worry—sowing under a star
that so loved a rock it begat snowshoe hares

and sugar maples, earthworms and swamp sparrows—
summer might go on and the first frost may never show,

and the heat shorting my mother's breath as she ambles
up the porch steps, the smoke slung wherever

the current carries it, will leave no place for her
on a warming planet, my mother who used to say

her plight was to live long and suffer, like sulfur
cosmos repeating themselves through the sidewalk—

we are doomed to survive—whose heart hums like wind in
dry reeds and now longs for more time

to pocket sea glass and slip her feet in the spilling
waves on a beach she's never been, where the world

will not end when she does, and I could go on
loving it all, I could, I could love it when she can't.

Island of Rabbits

To the west of Tripoli, an island once overbred

       with rabbits during the French Mandate

now has no rabbits and an UNESCO designation

       because an excavation revealed

baths from the 13th century and a freshwater well

       and the remains of a Crusader-era church

where people were massacred. It was a long time

       ago, but you can still see the places

they burrowed. The rabbits, I mean, though

       the people too wanted to live like a rabbit wants to live.

Hunger

Imaginary, the value of the pound, and yet when it drops
like an apple rotted from its branch, my family may starve.
1,507 pounds to the dollar. What that means if you're not
an economist: a kilogram of meat is now a luxury. A line
huddles outside a Beirut bakery though the price of subsidized
bread is up again. The worst financial crisis in 150 years,
the World Bank says. And I don't see the story anywhere
here. In my house with its lights on. Where I choose to skip
meals. Once we were stitched together by food stamps.
Dirt poor, my mother describes it, though land is more valuable
than almost anything. America and its incongruent abundance:
fields of corn and the hungry in the streets. The cattle well fed.
Security guards in grocery stores. If you die from hunger, the spirit
goes searching for food and the wanting never stops. Hard to say
what you'd do to live. My father picked an apple from someone's
tree, was chased until he dropped it. If you steal an apple, it's a crime.
If you withhold an apple from someone who's hungry, it's not.

The Bull of Heaven

Drought never stampedes—
all the rain has to do
is stop coming.
Maybe you already
knew this: it only takes
six rainless days,
and in Lebanon,
it means just
seventeen inches of rain
since September.
No rivers or wells
to fill with rainwater—
farmers will have to dig
to sate their crops,
if there's any
groundwater left.
When did you last
have to remember
water, blue
like a dream so real you
wake up crying?
I'm told King Soloman
built his temple
from our cedars,
and in its innermost
room, God rested.
Which prophet
begged the sky

and was promised
nothing? When the fields
parch, you'll know.
Wake up
now, the cedars
are burning.
The same forest
where the old gods slept.
The thing about
the end is you never
see it coming.

The Little Ice Age of Hard Truths

When the glaciers shifted and the Baltic Sea
froze over twice, when the crops ceded and
the livestock starved and the pathogens spread,
few people blamed the boot on their necks
for the bread cobbled from ground nutshells
when grain refused to grow, for the milk-emptied
cows swaying in the frost all night. No, when
drought clawed and children fevered in their sleep,
only hunting the most vulnerable would do,
to round up widows and call them witches,
to invade and raze, to burn, to bleed—it's true,
what people will do to each other under the banner
of God. You might even surprise yourself by who
you could be convinced to sacrifice.

Where the Music Goes

Floating along the emptiness of space,
the song of the ortolan bunting,
common crane, black-capped

chickadee is a minor third.
You would think it's made
to please us, the leaping

notes, like how we took hoofbeats
and made rhythm. We could dance
to anything: laundry kicking

around in the dryer. Rain
coming down. Swaying in the dread
of another Sunday.

We've outlived the final winter somehow.
We would've told our children
about the border canaries,

their small lamplight
in the mouth of the earth.
Yes, we sent them down

even though they might die.
They had been useful—
even their last song was beautiful.

My Love and I In the Shower, Contemplating the End

Maybe an asteroid, quick like a bomb going off. Suds
gracing your shoulders, oh, you're regal when you talk

obliteration, baby. One extinction for another.
It wouldn't be so bad to go like that. I just want

it to be painless. In eight years, 1997 XF11 could turn
everything in 200 miles to ash. Maybe bacteria survive.

Dust clouds would get the rest of us, or waves, or the boiling
ocean. Would you rather burn or freeze? It takes so little

to exterminate life on earth. A dwarf planet colliding with us.
A spark in the Higgs field that grows at the speed of light.

One formidable pandemic. Some real doomsday shit. It's good
that life is fragile, you say, picking up my dropped razor.

So we value it. But I don't want to hold dear the ephemeral.
Another scrub jay hiding its food to delight in later.

You say the world was not designed for permanence.
It's a huge space fluke meant to leave you wanting.

Like steam in the air after the shower's off. Like my
hands remembering your body long after you've gone.

How to Lucid Dream

My dead dogs float
like dandelion seeds to be near me,

their faces on my face, one miraculous
beast. In the beginning there was something

more than humans. God existed alone
in eternity and said, *Be*.

On Wednesday, there were angels.
On Thursday, the jinn.

The world rests on the back of a bull, the fin of a fish.
It explains the stampeding and swimming.

Here my love
is unfamiliar. Push a finger

through my palm.
Behold my feral face in the mirror.

This is where wind comes from:
between sleep and wake

where the dead are not really dead.
An eternity of almost touching.

Where Is Yazbek?

In front of the water, my love,
bright as a beach ball!

Loud as a dinner bell!
Sweet as a fig!

I'm finding new ways to mourn
the lives I didn't live.

And Teta is dying,
gone to the mountains

to haunt my ring
and divine the Turkish

grounds in my cup.
I wish you weren't dead!

I wish you weren't dead!

Let my future appear
like a lover's hands.

Like a face framed
by train window

and open the heart.
Before she died,

she fevered with visions:
Where is Yazbek?
Here, the cup says, a kettle, a journey,
a pear. You'll have success in the city,

a whole rabbit of it. A saw
to split brother from brother.

A great wheel at the cusp,
you're traveling somewhere soon.

A mountain for your joy, as much
as your palms can carry—

old friends will gather and
you'll gossip over argileh smoke

and your days of being
immune to wonder

are over,
just like that.

Take Me with You to the Mountains

Is it true the dead are so modest
they require a shroud I'm dying
to know if privacy is even a thing
when you're everywhere I read
we call our afterlife Akhirah and
our heaven Jannah there is no
sadness there I can't imagine
a life without sadness what else
could bring you to your knees
and would I miss the sharpness
either way you're in a grave
until the Day of Judgment
facing the Qibla three handfuls
of dirt three days of mourning
did you know your daughters
weren't at your procession and
did it hurt even if it's custom
my father watched his brother carry
your body from his phone's small
screen that's what happens when
you die in a pandemic an ocean
away his grief rippling out through
waves and satellites did you like
America and did it hurt you
that my father never came home
did you ever love him like you loved
his brother Teta it's so hard to be mad
at the dead I think my father will

mourn you until he's gone when
he talks about you he does so like
he's telling me about a person
I've never met and it hurts if only
because it feels true I feel your hand
on my spine to straighten my posture
you insisted I should be beautiful at all
times I was just a kid and didn't understand
beauty I still don't I kissed your hair
and smelled mint I kissed your soft
cheek I held your soft hands I didn't
know I would never see you again

Years We Lived Close to the Bone

When the dog died, I woke up with a mouth
full of fur. I think she would get a kick out of that,
but it takes hours to will myself from bed.
More to endure the morning, to not
fill her bowl or carry her to the yard
where she'd muster a few three-legged steps
before plopping down, exhausted, and I'd lift
her to my shoulder, her big, disappointed eyes like,
Can you believe this shit?

The way our bodies just give up?

She is more than just an animal.
How do I tell you I held her every day
of her life, that caring for one small dog
made me live when I didn't want to live?
I listen now for her scold of a bark,
follow the sound, follow the sound
into another day and do it all over again.

The Only World in Which the Dog Lives

Is in correspondence with the representatives of BarkBox: Did Bowie
enjoy the lamb jerky? And so I lie like I've been asked something
important: she pawed my calf for more! She climbed into the box
like a Christmas card. She soared through the air like a trapeze artist!
Can you believe it? My Bowie. Marching through the summer grass
up to her neck! Sun-footing through the brambles and the ivy! Little
solar flare bear in her hibernation sweater. You should see the snow
on her fur—it almost sparkled. A feather in her mouth, a flock.
Brought the wind with her, too. The whole house storming, fur
tumbleweeding down the hallway. Yes, her favorite toys are small
and yellow. Yes, I did know dogs can see the color yellow.
Yes, it is unhinged to pretend like this. Yes, I can hold.

When Capitalism Gets Me Down, I Remember

All souls have the same afterlife,
and your small days of
waking and working
and sleeping have no bearing
on the world to come.

Mother Of

The last voice her patients hear, unless we count
the heart monitor. It used to make her cry, zipping
up the body bags, but now there are too many and she
can't do both. When she calls me, she says no one thinks
of the nurses. The hospital ran out of PPE and she had to
wear trash bags over her scrubs. The antibacterial foam peels
back the skin of her fingertips. The discs in her spine fuse
until she winces when she walks. All that lifting and hauling.
And turning and proning. And hurrying and checking. No one
thinks of my mother dwindling with the ventilators.
My mother with the patient whose lungs burn for air.
She says it's like breathing underwater. A moral injury in that
the mind and hands act in opposition. One cries and one zips.

Love Letter #36

Let us continue
our version of life on earth.
Drink the dust poured
by our sad, smiling families.
Everyone will mourn
you, even the moon
who watched you
when no one else would.

Poem of Beginnings

The green earth yawned. The babies cried in gluey cocoons, aware
at once of the difficulty of having a body that rides through space
on a warm rock. A rock! It was downhill from there. Everything
was hard and we all lost our minds. We bottled water, for fuck's sake.
Flung the barn doors and burnt the hay. You know someone is telling
the truth when they're on fire. I thumb the hot stove moments too long.
Because I am an untold number of electrical currents away from being
dog food. The graffiti sprawling the overpass says CRUELTY IS
THE POINT. The babies agree. I am sick of towing my body around,
showing it the strange world like a newborn. All this wonder and nowhere
to rest. HAVE YOU SEEN MY HEART? the lost dog flyer taped
to the streetlamp asks. Oh, Heart, you're needed back home.
Boughs and blossoms trailing you like a wedding.
The moon and you have some explaining to do.

When Grief Made Us

In the new year, the ghosts show up.
   The family down the street cheers

because it was not their turn to be haunted.
   They do the neighborly thing

and ask if I need anything. Then they stop
   coming around and it's a little worse.

Of course I tried to outrun my fate. At first I shut
   the windows and pulled the curtains.

But when sleet plucked the glass and I could no longer
   stand the chatter of their teeth,

I opened the door. They touch each picture frame
   with their blue hands. They insist

TV static is better than the quiet. Every night
   is a tornado siren. From civil dawn to civil dusk.

I make long lists of what to do next.
   When my hair falls out again, they touch

the silk-white of my scalp. Tender as a mother. Holding my feet
   when I am too sad to move from the couch.

Moral Inventory

What good is your goodness really
if it is undone as soon as it begins?
I flew over an ocean slicked with plastic.
I am still afraid of whales even though I know
they are choking on our trash.
I had money in my pocket from a job
of casual corporate unkindness
and gave it to anyone who asked.
I want to be a better animal.
I want to love what I can while I can:
my dogs who cotton the grass,
a song that fills my cup and gallops me
under a hunter's moon. So what if I
snag in her antlers? I once had a body
that wasn't a body—it was a voice
in a god's mouth. It was the holy vowel.
Oh, animal, I thank you.
Oh, flank, oh, wanting gut,
say it matters. Tell me to begin
again. Tell me, and I will.

Notes

The title of this collection and a line from "In the gloaming, in the roiling night" take inspiration from Anne Carson's *The Autobiography of Red:* "Stesichoros released being. All the substances in the world went floating up. Suddenly there was nothing to interfere with horses being *hollow hooved*. Or a river being *root silver*. Or a child *bruiseless*. Or hell *as deep as the sun is high*. Or Herakles *ordeal strong*. Or a planet *middle night stuck*. Or an insomniac *outside the joy*."

"In the gloaming, in the roiling night" also evokes Lucille Clifton's poem "won't you celebrate with me" with the line "let me spring from the jaws of what tried to kill me."

Acknowledgements

My deepest gratitude to the editors at the following journals who gave these poems a home, often in earlier forms and/or under different titles:

32 Poems: "Hunger"

The Academy of American Poets' *Poem-a-Day*: "In the gloaming, in the roiling night"

The Adroit Journal: "Take Me with You to the Mountains," "Mother Of [God bless…]," and "The Chariot"

The Atlantic: "Reasons to Live"

Bear Review: "Forgiveness" and "The Wolf Tells the Magpie"

The Believer: "We don't talk about the children until we do"

Copper Nickel: "Standard Candle"

Cordite Poetry Review: "Years We Lived Close to the Bone"

Diode: "Shame, Abridged"

Glass Poetry: "The Sleepwalker"

Honey Literary: "How to Lucid Dream," "The Only World in Which the Dog Lives," and "The Jinn Who Loved Me"

Kenyon Review: "All the Oranges of Tripoli" and "Guilt Me"

The Journal: "The one where I beg"

Lickety Split: "Love Letter #36"

Ninth Letter: "Bull of Heaven"

Magma Poetry: "The Little Ice Age of Hard Truths"

The Margins: "The Sarah Poems" and "Poem of Beginnings"

One: "Nocturne with Teeth"

Pleiades: "Catalog of the Inalienable"

Poetry Magazine: "The Years of Water & Light"

Poetry Northwest: "Mother of [Paintbrushes]" and "The Happiest People on Earth"

Prairie Schooner: "Where Is Yazbek?" and "Island of Rabbits"

The Rumpus: "Amor Fati" and "Guns Won't Feed You, But Hold Out Your Hands"

The Shallow Ends: "Everything Will Hurt for a While"

The Spectacle: "Learning Arabic" and "After the Argument"

Southern Indiana Review: "The Heart Is Another Country" and

"Mother Of [Forgetting]"

Sugar House Review: "Mother Of [An ascending thoracic]" and "When Grief Made Us"

VIDA Review: "Men Compliment Me" and "Origin"

WILDNESS: "Moral Inventory"

"Reasons to Live" appeared in the anthology *You Are Here: Poetry in the Natural World* edited by US Poet Laureate Ada Limón and published in association with the Library of Congress.

"In the gloaming, in the roiling night," "The Years of Water & Light," and "Guilt Me" were reprinted in the anthology *In the Tempered Dark: Contemporary Poets Transcending Elegy* edited by Lisa Fay Coutley.

"The Sleepwalker," "Amor Fati," and "The one where I beg" were reprinted in the anthology *We Call to the Eye and the Night: Love Poems by Writers of Arab Heritage* edited by Hala Alyan and Zeina Hashem Beck.

Thank you to the National Endowment for the Arts for the fellowship that supported the creation of this collection, to the Ohio Arts Council for its support of my work, the Sundress Academy for the Arts for the residency that gave me time to write, and to the Kenyon Review for the Peter Taylor Fellowship that helped me grow these poems.

Thank you to my mother for letting me share a piece of her with you. To my sister Sarah for being my first reader and for making me better. To my sisters Mariam and Courtney, my father and Lisa, and Rafael for your support. To Kathryn Potraz, Kristen Pietras, Maggie Derethik, Gary Lovely, Adam Hong, and James Darbee for being my third space.

Thank you, Kirsten Reach, for your thoughtful edits that guided earlier versions of this collection. Maggie Smith, Elissa Washuta, Saeed Jones, Keith Leonard, Mandy Shunnarah, Eugene Rutigliano, Marcus Jackson, Rachel Mennies, Scott Woods, Elizabeth Dark, Victoria Chang, Adrian Matejka, Ilya Kaminsky, Ron Mitchell, Marcus Wicker, Will Evans, Ada Limón, David Baker, Allison Joseph, and the late Jon Tribble, thank you for everything you've taught me.

Thank you to my brilliant editor Chet Weise and everyone at Third Man Books for bringing these poems into the world.

To my dogs Penny, Rosemary, Winnie, and Henry, who sat patiently through every draft. And to Eric Shonkwiler, my muse, my home.

About the Author

Photo by Megan Leigh Barnard

Ruth Awad is a Lebanese American poet, 2021 National Endowment for the Arts Poetry Fellow, and the author of *Set to Music a Wildfire*, winner of the 2016 Michael Waters Poetry Prize and the 2018 Ohioana Book Award for Poetry. Alongside Rachel Mennies, she is the co-editor of *The Familiar Wild: On Dogs & Poetry*. She is the recipient of a 2020 and 2016 Ohio Arts Council Individual Excellence Award. Widely anthologized, her poems most recently appear in *You Are Here: Poetry in the Natural World* edited by US Poet Laureate Ada Limón and published in association with the Library of Congress. Her work appears in *The Atlantic, Poetry, Poem-a-Day, AGNI, The Believer, New Republic, Kenyon Review, Pleiades, Missouri Review, The Rumpus*, and elsewhere. She lives in Columbus, Ohio.

Printed in the USA
CPSIA information can be obtained
at www.ICGtesting.com
JSHW010738140724
66374JS00006B/6